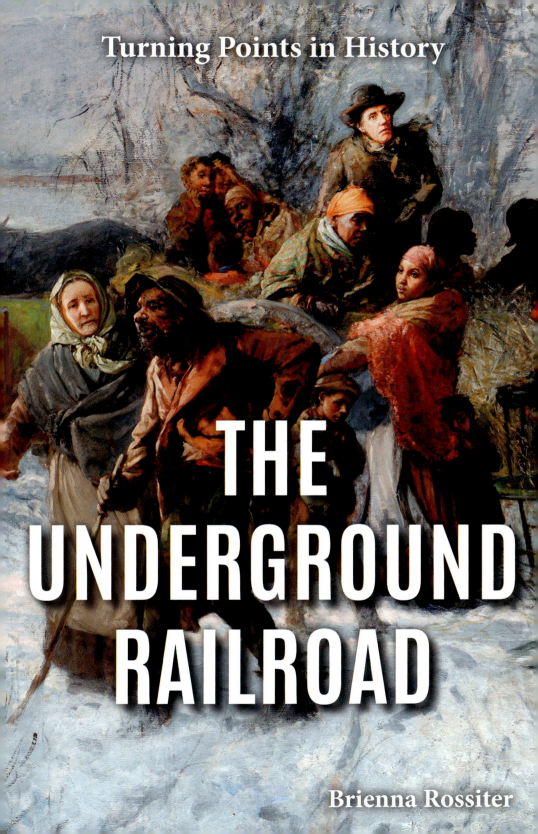

Turning Points in History

THE UNDERGROUND RAILROAD

Brienna Rossiter

WWW.APEXEDITIONS.COM

Copyright © 2025 by Apex Editions, Mendota Heights, MN 55120. All rights reserved. No part of this book may be reproduced or utilized in any form or by any means without written permission from the publisher.

Apex is distributed by North Star Editions:
sales@northstareditions.com | 888-417-0195

Produced for Apex by Red Line Editorial.

Photographs ©: Art Collection 2/Alamy Stock Photo, cover, 1; Shutterstock Images, 4–5, 6–7, 8–9, 10–11, 18–19, 40–41, 42–43, 46–47; McPherson & Oliver/Library of Congress, 12–13; John Andrews/Library of Congress, 14–15; MPI/Archive Photos/Getty Images, 16–17; G. H. Loomis/Library of Congress, 20–21; Matt Rourke/AP Images, 22–23; National Park Service, 24–25; Fotosearch/Archive Photos/Getty Images, 26–27; Bentley Historical Library, 28–29; Interim Archives/Archive Photos/Getty Images, 30–31; New York Public Library, 32–33, 49, 50–51; Three Lions/Hulton Archive/Getty Images, 34–35; Armstead and White/Library of Congress/Corbis Historical/VCG/Getty Images, 36–37; Benjamin F. Powelson/Library of Congress, 39, 58; Bettmann/Getty Images, 44–45; John Moffat/Library of Congress, 52–53; B. F. Smith & Son/Library of Congress, 54–55; Library of Congress, 56–57

Library of Congress Control Number: 2024943631

ISBN
979-8-89250-466-9 (hardcover)
979-8-89250-482-9 (paperback)
979-8-89250-512-3 (ebook pdf)
979-8-89250-498-0 (hosted ebook)

Printed in the United States of America
Mankato, MN
012025

NOTE TO PARENTS AND EDUCATORS

Apex books are designed to build literacy skills in striving readers. Exciting, high-interest content attracts and holds readers' attention. The text is carefully leveled to allow students to achieve success quickly.

TABLE OF CONTENTS

Chapter 1
ESCAPE TO THE NORTH 4

Chapter 2
HISTORY 11

Chapter 3
A SECRET NETWORK 20

Chapter 4
RAILROAD CODE 30

Story Spotlight
HARRIET TUBMAN 38

Chapter 5
RISKY JOURNEY 40

Story Spotlight
WILLIAM STILL 48

Chapter 6
LASTING IMPACT 50

TIMELINE • 59
COMPREHENSION QUESTIONS • 60
GLOSSARY • 62
TO LEARN MORE • 63
ABOUT THE AUTHOR • 63
INDEX • 64

Chapter 1
ESCAPE TO THE NORTH

It was midnight on a Saturday in 1853. Four young Black men ran. One of them was named Wesley Harris. He led the other three. They were trying to escape enslavement. In about two days, they covered more than 60 miles (97 km).

Wesley Harris was enslaved in a town called Harpers Ferry.

Near a town in Maryland, a Black man warned them. He said the townspeople were not sympathetic. So, the men hid. But a farmer found them. He let them sleep in his barn.

The next day, the barn was surrounded by white men with guns. The farmer had betrayed them. A fight broke out. All four freedom seekers were captured. Three were sent to jail. But Harris was badly hurt. So, captors held him in a nearby building for weeks.

To reach freedom, a man named Henry Brown traveled for 27 hours inside a small crate.

However, a friend brought Harris some rope. A few days later, Harris escaped. He climbed out the window. Then he found shelter with a friend. After that, Harris continued north. Other people gave him a horse and medical care. He eventually reached Canada. Harris was finally free.

MANY METHODS

Freedom seekers traveled in many ways. Some fled on foot. Some stole horses and carriages. Others got rides on trains or ships. A few people even shipped themselves inside boxes. They were carried as freight. Friends at the other side of the journey opened the boxes.

Some enslaved people were kidnapped from their homes in Africa. Others were born to enslaved parents in the Americas.

Chapter 2
HISTORY

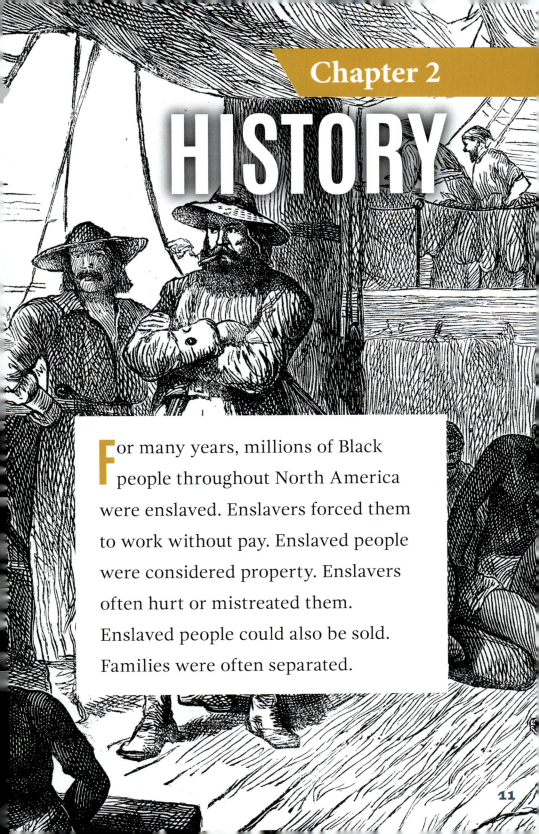

For many years, millions of Black people throughout North America were enslaved. Enslavers forced them to work without pay. Enslaved people were considered property. Enslavers often hurt or mistreated them. Enslaved people could also be sold. Families were often separated.

Many enslaved people tried to escape. Most fled on their own. But some got help from people who opposed slavery.

In the late 1700s, some US states began making slavery illegal. These were known as free states. Enslaved people often fled there. They hoped to find help and freedom.

FINDING FREEDOM

By 1804, slavery was illegal in most Northern states. But escapes began much earlier. For example, enslaved people had been fleeing to Florida since the 1600s. At that time, Spain ruled Florida. Black people found several ways to live freely there.

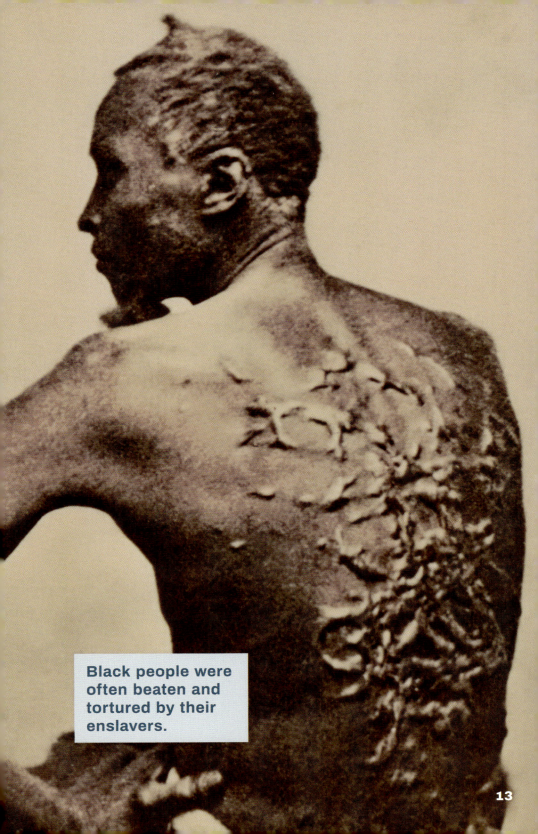

Black people were often beaten and tortured by their enslavers.

Anthony Burns escaped to the North, but his enslaver found him. Burns was forced to go back to slavery.

Enslavers didn't want people to escape. So, they made laws. One was part of the Northwest Ordinance. Another was in the US Constitution. People who escaped from slavery could be caught and sent back. This was true even in free areas.

The Fugitive Slave Act of 1793 did more. It said slave catchers didn't need proof that people had escaped. They could just say people did. Courts would decide if these claims were true. There would be no trials.

In response, Northern states passed their own laws. Some laws tried to help freedom seekers in court. Abolitionists also formed groups that helped with escapes.

So, enslavers created the Fugitive Slave Act of 1850. It made helping with escapes a serious crime. People could face large fines or jail time. They could even be charged with treason. The act said freedom seekers couldn't have trials or speak in court. It also said local law enforcement had to help capture them.

In 1858, people in Ohio rescued someone from a slave catcher. They were tried for breaking the Fugitive Slave Act of 1850.

Disagreements between Northern and Southern states over slavery eventually led to the US Civil War (1861–1865).

The act sparked outrage throughout the North. More people began opposing slavery. People also kept helping freedom seekers despite the risks. Many joined a group known as the Underground Railroad.

WRONGLY CAUGHT

Slave hunters often misused the Fugitive Slave Acts. They caught people who hadn't run away. Then they lied. They said the people had escaped from slavery. In many cases, judges chose to believe them.

Chapter 3

A SECRET NETWORK

The Underground Railroad wasn't a train. And it didn't go underground. Instead, it was a secret network. It helped people escape from slavery.

The Underground Railroad was mostly run by free Black people, such as Leonard Grimes.

The network began in the late 1700s. But it really took off in the 1830s and 1840s. At first, it was mainly run by free Black people and Quakers. Both groups often lived in Philadelphia, Pennsylvania, and other parts of New England.

EARLY ALLIES

The Quakers were a religious group. They believed all people were equal. So, they thought slavery was wrong. As early as the 1600s, they were working to end it. They tried to change laws. And they helped people escape.

Mother Bethel AME Church in Philadelphia was part of the Underground Railroad.

Over time, the network grew. It included many routes. They ran through 14 states and parts of Canada. People called these routes "lines." That word came from railroads. Trains were new and exciting in the 1800s.

Most routes led north. But some freedom seekers escaped to the West. Others traveled to Mexico. And some went to Florida. In Florida, they often lived with the Seminoles. These Indigenous people had been helping freedom seekers for many years.

Most lines began after people reached free states. Lines were also broken into sections. People stopped at safe houses along the way. These places were called "stations."

VIGILANCE COMMITTEES

Many Northern cities had vigilance committees. Abolitionists started these groups. They helped freedom seekers. Groups raised money. They found places for people to stay. They helped send messages, too. The groups also defended people from slave catchers.

Robert Purvis was an abolitionist. He led the vigilance committee in Philadelphia.

After he escaped from slavery, Henry Bibb started an antislavery newspaper in Canada.

After the 1850 Fugitive Slave Act, Canada became the most common destination. Slavery had been illegal there since 1834. US enslavers had no rights to recapture people there.

FREEDOM IN CANADA

British Canada had a few colonies. One was Upper Canada. Because of a 1793 law, any enslaved person who reached it became free. During the War of 1812 (1812–1815), US troops fought in Canada. Some US soldiers brought enslaved people with them. These people learned about the law. They told others back home.

Chapter 4
RAILROAD CODE

Escaping slavery was illegal. So was helping people escape. For this reason, people used code words. Freedom seekers were called "passengers," "cargo," or "freight." They traveled between cities called "terminals." Safe houses were "stations" or "depots."

Pro-slavery mobs sometimes destroyed places known to be safe houses.

"Station masters" were people who ran the safe houses. Some were white. But many were free Black people.

Station masters hid people in their homes or property. They helped plan and arrange travel to the next station, often by sending letters. Sometimes, they gave people money or supplies to help with their journey.

HIDING IN COFFINS

Henrietta S. Bowers Duterte was a famous station master. She worked as an undertaker. She sometimes hid freedom seekers in coffins.

Jermain Wesley Loguen ran a station from his home in New York. Like many station masters, he had escaped from slavery.

"Conductors" guided people from station to station. They traveled with passengers and showed the way. This job was very risky. If caught, conductors could be killed.

SMALL SECTIONS

Most conductors traveled just part of a route. This was partly for safety. If people knew the whole route, they might be forced to tell it. There was another reason, too. The Underground Railroad was not one big whole. It was made up of many small groups of people. They often worked independently.

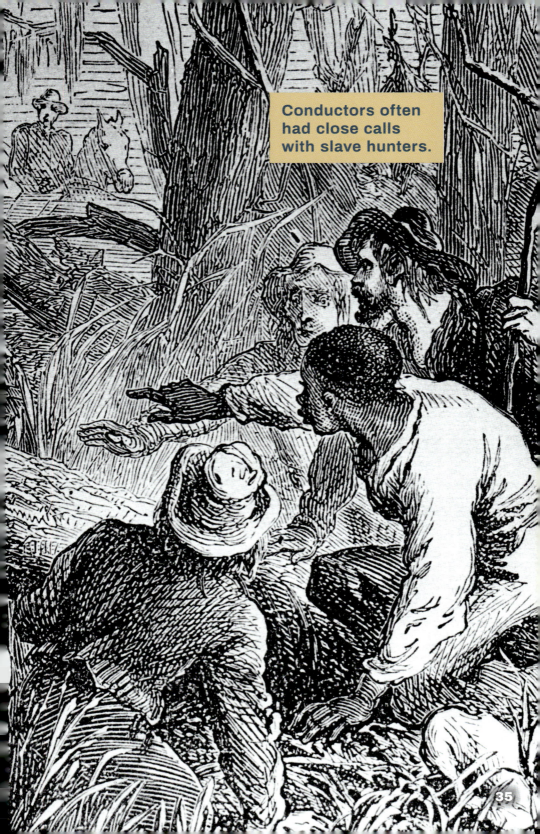
Conductors often had close calls with slave hunters.

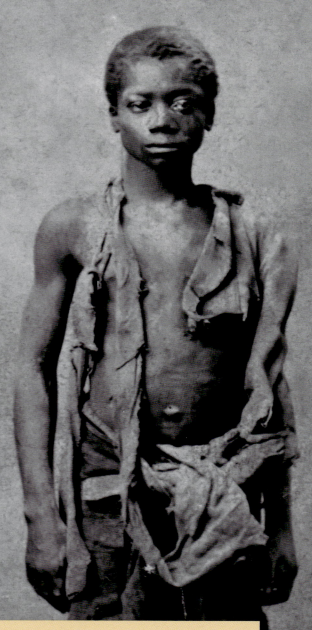

Worn-out clothes could make freedom seekers stand out and be easier to capture. So, helpers often gave them new clothes.

"Ticket agents" helped people plan journeys. They spread messages and information. To do this, they visited different people and places. So, many ticket agents had jobs that involved travel. Preachers and doctors were two examples. They used this work as a cover.

"Stockholders" gave money or supplies. Passengers needed food and clothing. Some also needed tickets for boats or trains. Groups raised money to buy these things.

Story Spotlight

HARRIET TUBMAN

Harriet Tubman was a conductor. Like many conductors, Tubman had escaped from slavery on her own. Her family was enslaved in Maryland. In 1849, she learned that the enslaver planned to sell her. So, she ran away. She fled to Pennsylvania.

Tubman returned to Maryland in December 1850. She guided three people to freedom. She made more than 10 more trips after that. She rescued dozens of people, including her parents. Most of these people went to Canada.

During the Civil War, Harriet Tubman was a spy for the Union Army.

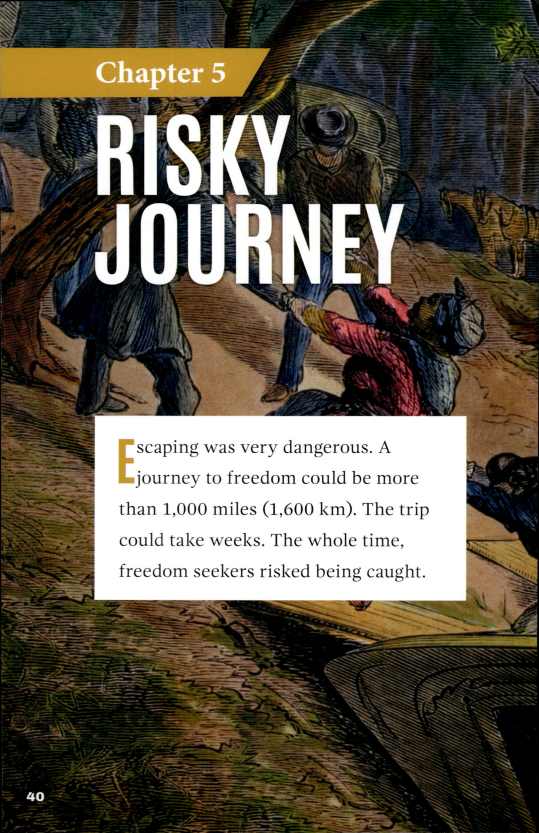

Chapter 5
RISKY JOURNEY

Escaping was very dangerous. A journey to freedom could be more than 1,000 miles (1,600 km). The trip could take weeks. The whole time, freedom seekers risked being caught.

Most freedom seekers were young men. But sometimes whole families fled together.

Some enslavers used dogs to find and catch people. They also hired people to watch common escape routes. Slave catchers patrolled cities and borders. People even checked ships and trains for freedom seekers who might be hiding.

ESCAPE ROUTES
Near free states, people often ran north. They tried to cross borders. But many freedom seekers went to ports. From there, they could take ships. Many free Black men worked as sailors. They often helped people escape.

Freedom seekers sometimes had to fight slave catchers.

Enslavers also offered rewards. So, some people pretended to help freedom seekers. Then they betrayed them for the money.

ESCAPE ADS

When people escaped, enslavers posted ads in newspapers. The ads described the freedom seekers. And they offered rewards for bringing them back. Ads printed every day but Sunday. So, people often fled on Saturday nights. That left more time to get away.

> Around 200,000 ads about people who had escaped from slavery were printed in US newspapers.

REWARD!

NAWAY

...dersigned, living on Current ...welve miles above Doniphan, ..., on 2nd of March, 1860, A N ...A N, about 30 years old, weighs about ...ad, with a scar on it; had on brown pants and coat ...old black wool hat; shoes size No. 11.

...ill be given to any person who may apprehend this ...rehended in this State outside of Ripley county, or $25 if taken in Ripley county.

APOS TUCKER.

Freedom seekers usually traveled at night. They rested and hid during the day. Helpers often gave freedom seekers rides in wagons. Helpers hid them beneath piles of hay or goods. Many freedom seekers rode ships. Crew members often helped them.

If caught, freedom seekers often faced terrible punishment. Enslavers would beat them brutally, sell them, or even kill them. Enslavers wanted to scare others into not escaping.

Stations on the Underground Railroad could be 10 to 20 miles (16 to 32 km) apart. People often had to travel through rain and cold.

Story Spotlight

WILLIAM STILL

William Still was a famous abolitionist. He was born free. But both of his parents had been enslaved.

Still lived in Philadelphia for many years. He ran a station there. More than 640 people stopped at it on their way to Canada. Still kept a record of everyone who came to his station. He saved letters people wrote, too. In 1872, he published these details in a book. It was called *The Underground Railroad*. The book became famous around the world.

William Still worked to help Black Americans gain freedom and equal rights.

Chapter 6
LASTING IMPACT

Risks continued after the journey ended. People could still be captured or betrayed. Slave catchers often came to Northern states. Some even went to Canada. They tried to capture people there even though that was illegal.

William Still's mother, Charity, was kidnapped and enslaved again after escaping. Then she escaped a second time.

Freedom seekers often had to deal with discrimination in their new homes. Some places had limits on where Black people could live, work, or attend school. Many freedom seekers spoke out. They called for equal rights. They also helped one another find jobs and education.

THE POWER OF STORIES
Several people wrote books about their escapes from slavery. They described the dangers they faced. And they told of the pain they suffered while enslaved. These books showed how awful slavery was. They also helped disprove the common lie that Black people couldn't be independent.

Josiah Henson escaped from slavery in 1830. He started a town for others who had escaped.

Frederick Douglass was an abolitionist and an early supporter of women's right to vote.

No one knows how many people the Underground Railroad helped. Estimates range from 25,000 to 100,000 people. That's low compared to the total number of enslaved people. Even so, the Underground Railroad had a major impact.

FREDERICK DOUGLASS

Frederick Douglass escaped from slavery in 1838. He wrote a book about his experiences. Later, he became a station master. He used his home in New York. For many years, Douglass traveled and spoke. He called for change to help Black Americans be treated equally.

The Underground Railroad's passengers showed great skills and bravery. So did the people who helped them. Many people from both groups helped the Union Army in the US Civil War (1861–1865). Many also helped change people's minds about slavery.

Congress ended both Fugitive Slave Acts in 1864. And in 1865, the United States officially ended slavery. But people didn't stop working to help Black Americans gain equal rights and freedoms.

About 179,000 Black soldiers fought for the Union Army. Nearly 40,000 of them died in that fight for freedom.

TIMELINE

JULY 2, 1777 — Vermont becomes the first place in the United States to make slavery illegal.

JULY 13, 1787 — The US government passes the Northwest Ordinance. This law gives enslavers permission to capture freedom seekers.

FEBRUARY 12, 1793 — Congress passes the Fugitive Slave Act of 1793. It gives courts the power to decide if people accused of escaping slavery are guilty.

JULY 9, 1793 — Upper Canada, a British colony, passes the Act to Limit Slavery. As a result, any enslaved person who reaches the colony becomes free.

AUGUST 1, 1834 — Slavery becomes illegal in all of the British Empire, including Canada.

SEPTEMBER 18, 1850 — Congress passes the Fugitive Slave Act of 1850. This law adds harsher punishment for people who help freedom seekers.

DECEMBER 6, 1865 — The Thirteenth Amendment to the Constitution declares an official end to slavery in the United States.

1872 — William Still publishes the first edition of *The Underground Railroad*.

COMPREHENSION QUESTIONS

Write your answers on a separate piece of paper.

1. Write a few sentences describing what the Underground Railroad was.

2. What is one fact about the Underground Railroad that surprised you? Why?

3. Where did most Underground Railroad lines begin?

    A. in slave states

    B. in free states

    C. in Canada

4. Why would freedom seekers still be at risk after they reached free states?

    A. Free states still allowed slavery.

    B. US laws let slave catchers capture people in any state.

    C. US laws required freedom seekers to go to Canada.

5. What does **ports** mean in this book?

   *But many freedom seekers went to **ports**. From there, they could take ships.*

   A. parts of machines where cords can attach
   B. areas near rivers, bays, or other types of water
   C. areas far from rivers, bays, or other types of water

6. What does **discrimination** mean in this book?

   *Freedom seekers often had to deal with **discrimination** in their new homes. Some places had limits on where Black people could live, work, or attend school.*

   A. unfair treatment because of who people are or how they look
   B. enslavement after being free for a period of time
   C. fancy houses where wealthy people lived

Answer key on page 64.

GLOSSARY

abolitionists
People who worked to end slavery.

betrayed
Hurt a person or group by giving help or information to their enemies or opponents.

colonies
Areas that are ruled by a different country.

Constitution
The document that tells the basic laws and beliefs of the United States.

freight
Goods carried by ships, trains, or trucks.

fugitive
A person who is running away or hiding, often to avoid arrest or capture.

Indigenous
Related to the original people who lived in an area.

involved
Had something as a usual part or task.

patrolled
Moved throughout an area, watching it closely.

treason
The crime of helping an enemy of one's country.

vigilance
Paying close attention in order to stay safe.

TO LEARN MORE
BOOKS

Ahrens, Niki. *Harriet Tubman: Abolitionist and American Hero.* Minneapolis: Lerner Publications, 2022.

Tyner, Dr. Artika R. *The Untold Story of John P. Parker: Underground Railroad Conductor.* North Mankato, MN: Capstone Press, 2024.

Williams, Carla. *The Underground Railroad.* Mankato, MN: The Child's World, 2022.

ONLINE RESOURCES

Visit **www.apexeditions.com** to find links and resources related to this title.

ABOUT THE AUTHOR

Brienna Rossiter is a writer and editor who lives in Minnesota.

INDEX

abolitionists, 16, 26, 48

Canada, 9, 24, 29, 38, 48, 50
conductors, 34, 38

Douglass, Frederick, 55

Florida, 12, 24
free Black people, 22, 32, 42
free states, 12, 26, 42
Fugitive Slave Act of 1793, 15, 19, 56
Fugitive Slave Act of 1850, 16, 19, 29, 56

Harris, Wesley, 4, 6, 9

lines, 24, 26

Maryland, 6, 38

New England, 22
New York, 55
Northwest Ordinance, 15

passengers, 30, 34, 37, 56
Philadelphia, Pennsylvania, 22, 48

Quakers, 22

Seminoles, 24
ships, 9, 42, 46
slave catchers, 15, 19, 26, 42, 50
station masters, 32, 48, 55
stations, 26, 30, 32, 34, 48
Still, William, 48
stockholders, 37

ticket agents, 37
trains, 9, 20, 24, 37, 42
Tubman, Harriet, 38

Underground Railroad, The, 48
US Civil War, 56

vigilance committees, 26

ANSWER KEY:
1. Answers will vary; 2. Answers will vary; 3. B; 4. B; 5. B; 6. A